HIDDEN PLAIN SIGHT

A Prepper's Guide to Hiding, Discovering, and Scavenging Diversion Safes and Caches

Matthew Dermody

Table of Contents

ACKNOWLEDGEMENTS:

I would like to thank my friends, fans, and readership who have contributed some of the photos featured throughout this book, especially to Jake Lang for the utility marker photos. All other photos are my own or appear courtesy of www.pixabay.com

Special thanks to Dan Ingram of New Jersey Concealment Furniture for granting permission to use some of the photographs of the high quality concealment furniture that he constructs.

No acknowledgement section would be complete without the inclusion of my wonderful wife and our twin girls. Their faithful support and encouragement are essential to my writing success. I love you very much.

Foreword:

A Word of Caution to Law Enforcement

The role of today's modern police officer is under tremendous scrutiny. Every move, decision, and response to a dispatched call is recorded, analyzed, and watched countless times to call into question an officer's motives, training, tactics, and character. People who were neither in their position at the time nor ever subjected to the split-second, life-or-death decision making process, are allowed to second-guess and scrutinize events without full possession of the facts, preponderance of the evidence, or objectivity.

It is not an easy job. He is picked apart by peers, superiors, bureaucrats, politicians, and citizenry who are either out-of-touch with the concepts of modern policing, ignorant of case law and/or police procedures, or deceived by the inaccurate portrayals of law enforcement on prime time television. Every day, he is subjected to abuse and to the fear of a departmental lack of confidence in his ability to do his job safely and effectively, in addition to the lack of respect and representation from lawmakers and elected officials who are more concerned with retaining their office, rather than retaining good officers.

He repeatedly sees his efforts to rid the streets of crime unrewarded by the apathy of citizens in society who have no desire or moral compunction to change their neighborhoods. Prosecutors invalidate his bravery and valor with plea bargains and defense attorneys mock his dedication by transferring the victimhood from the actual victim to the perpetrator. His professional discretion is curtailed and stifled by crippling rules of engagement, outdated/ineffective procedures, and mandatory protocols. He is now placed in a position of disadvantage, as criminals have neither the desire nor obligation to play by the rules of civilized society.

There is no doubt that several of society's institutions are in desperate need of reform and restructuring. Law enforcement and modern policing are neither exempt nor immune as the pool of potential officer candidates are pulled from the very society that begat them. When proper history and the Constitution are no longer taught, how can we expect our new law enforcement officers to honor and uphold something of which they have very little knowledge or understanding?

There is a time to which we as a society and lovers of freedom, the rule of law, and the United States Constitution, must return.

I empathize with the modern police officer. My father was a police officer for 27 years. I am a military veteran, I have a college degree in Criminal

Justice, and I have worked in various fields directly assisting with police officers. The amount of respect I have for military veterans and police is tremendous. Despite all of this, I sincerely implore any law enforcement officer reading this book to reacquaint themselves with the oath they swore to uphold. You have sworn an Oath of Honor to uphold the Constitution, your community, and the agency you serve.

We have seen the slow invasion and infringement upon many of our once inalienable rights by politicians and lawmakers who have forgotten or ignored their oaths of office, who then sit back and watch as we now must enforce laws we know are not lawful or constitutional. Some laws are so bad that we don't need the Supreme Court's ruling to tell us how overreaching and bad they are, yet we are imprisoned by the power of a paycheck.

As you absorb the information presented in this book, it is my hope that my admonition does not fall on deaf ears and hardened hearts. It is not, nor should it be, a crime for people to stockpile supplies, prepare for disasters, or protect assets. People who employ the methods and means described within this book may not be criminals.

I hope this will serve as a sober warning to any police officer or agent assigned to the collection or confiscation of a citizens' property. You will inevitably contact persons reluctant and even openly hostile to your attempts to separate them from their property. They will attempt to use deadly force, particularly when dealing with firearms confiscation.

You, as a police officer, had better be DAMN sure, both in your confidence and in obedience to the orders that you give or receive; as well as your own personal convictions. You must also be prepared for the fury and fight that some individuals will unleash upon you and your colleagues. Thoughtful and deeply sincere consideration needs to occur in order for you to justify the deliberate entering into harm's way just to follow orders or receive a paycheck.

If your desire is to return safely home at the end of your shift, property confiscation orders are going to be in direct opposition to your desires. I mourn the officers who lose their lives in the line of duty and empathize with their families. However, I will not bestow valor for sacrifice when common sense should have been soberly donned in the same manner as a ballistic vest and body armor.

If you, or those whom you have authority over, proceed in property confiscation, that shift goal may not be reached. Families of fallen officers will find little to no comfort in life insurance policies or moving eulogies; when all they want is a spouse to hold them and to make sure children have a mother or father present. Paychecks are only available if you're alive to receive and deposit those checks. If you stop existing, the checks stop coming, too.

This is not a threat, nor is it intended as such. Your family needs you and the protections you provide to them. Attempting to take away any citizens' right to protect themselves, their families, and their property, may leave your family unprotected and vulnerable should any edict to disarm or forcefully separate property/possessions from citizens be put into action. Consequently, it also makes you a traitor to your oath and to your fellow citizen of this great country.

To all my law enforcement friends for whom I have the highest respect, it is my hope and earnest prayer that you will be steadfast and faithful to your sworn oath, always choosing what is morally right and that which secures, defends, and honors the rights of the people listed by the Constitution of the United States of America.

"Sometimes the best hiding place is the one that's in plain sight."

- Stephanie Meyer

Chapter 1:
Reasons Why People Hoard and Hide Possessions

In order to understand the lengths people go to hide their personal belongings, it is necessary to have a basic knowledge as to why they do so. Some things are just meant to stay out of sight from prying eyes. Legislation and technology are swiftly drilling holes into the hull of personal privacy. Similar to the *Titanic*, the Bill of Rights was once considered the unsinkable behemoth of our nation's republic. Some may argue that the Bill of Rights has already hit several legislative "icebergs" and in now taking on water, with no hope of restoring its' once watertight integrity to keep it afloat.

No longer are enemies of personal freedom confined to the limitations of large, conspicuous surveillance and recording devices. Today, everyone carries a video and voice recorder: the mobile smart phone.   With it, conversations once considered private, can be broadcast over the Internet in a matter of minutes, destroying a person's privacy, or even worse, their reputation, dignity, and honor.

One need not look any further than the nightly news in the past months and years and watch as uninformed, mindless minions march for the rights of someone else to be stripped away. Little do they know or even care that the very rights they protest against are the very rights that ensure their ability to protest in the first place.

It is events such as these, unfolding before our eyes each night on the news, that cause people to proactively plan and prepare for troubled days. People are looking to maintain some semblance of control in uncertain times and it often manifests itself by storing up essential supplies when the time comes when those items are too hard to find, become too expensive, become illegal to possess, or are no longer available.

An old Mason jar full of coins is a common find in many households, but many Americans have other substantial provisions secretly stored. Photo courtesy of www.pixabay.com.

One of the purposes of this book is to highlight one of the oldest and most ingenious hiding places for whatever one considers valuable ever devised: the diversion safe. A diversion safe is a constructed or modified hiding place that has the outward appearance of a commonplace item while secretly containing an accessible compartment in which valuables or contraband are hidden from sight.

One of the diversion safes' most alluring benefits stem from the amount of time burglars spend inside a home looking for valuables to steal. According to information provided by the FBI on crime statistics, burglars typically spend less than five minutes inside a residential home.[1] The longer the intruder stays in the home, his chances of being discovered increases greatly, being confronted, and/or being shot by the homeowner.

Most burglaries are committed by opportunists looking for valuables rather than confrontations, so most attempts occur when the legal occupants are least likely to be there. This, however, is no guarantee of unlimited "browsing down the aisles" as if at the local store. Residential alarm systems are much more affordable and are no longer found exclusively among the financially affluent suburbs.

As I have confessed in some of my other books, I love hiding things. The only reasonable explanation I can offer for the behavior is that I grew up with younger siblings and shared a bedroom until I was a teenager. In order to protect my toys or belongings, I had to take adequate measures to ensure that the things I considered private and valuable, were hidden from my younger brothers.

Let's look at some of the most common reasons people hide belongings.

1. Personal Safety

Unfortunately, we live in a world where there are people possessing limited amounts or completely devoid of common sense, decency, and strong moral convictions. While this can be contributed to any number of factors such as single parent households, lack of religion, no discipline at home, the list goes on and on. The bottom line is that people prey upon other people. They hurt others. They lie and manipulate others with little regard for whom they hurt or how they hurt them for personal gain. In return, we are suspicious of others and hide things that may make it difficult to maintain the status quo of our own self-preservation. We hide cash and jewelry from the strung-out spouse or roommate who cares more about his next fix than the upcoming rent.

The old saying, "Knowledge is power" and sometimes having the power of knowledge puts one at risk by those who want that knowledge suppressed or destroyed as it threatens the power obtained by some ruling elite or government. This is the plot scenario of countless books and movies because it mirrors the realities of the world in which we live.

How often do we hear of events or scandals being revealed to the masses after someone mysteriously dies? Their wish is to expose some injustice or corruption, but their untimely death results in no testimonies, no convictions, and no justice. The body counts are the lubrication poured into the ever-churning engine of a villainous, corporate/political machine. After a certain disgraced Senator was found to be in possession of hundreds of thousands of emails in a computer folder labeled "Life Insurance", we can often extrapolate out what that may mean from a personal safety perspective.[2] Much more intriguing is how they ended up there. Could another been seeking the protection, choosing to hide it on a device other than their own?

2. Avoid Embarrassment

There are a number of vices and secret sins that people wish to avoid public disclosure or discovery by other family members. I could describe all of these within this category, but I don't feel it necessary. I would merely suggest, thinking about something that you have tucked away that you would not want your children, your spouse, even your pastor or priest to see. Without going into any sordid description of any one item, one understands both the gravity and reasoning behind keeping things hidden. This is not an exclusive, males-only behavior.

3. Avoid contraband detection

As we grow, especially during our teen years, we desire and seek the capacity for earning/gaining more independence. As the ability to make more of our own choices grows, experimentation with things expressly forbidden or restricted/illegal to possess seems both a natural and unavoidable path. There are very few of us who never employed a secret hiding place for things that we were forbidden to have in our possession either by parents, law enforcement, or by both.

4. Create surplus

One can hardly go far into the prepper and survivalist culture of self-reliance without running into the subject of gear caches and doomsday stockpiles. Having a cache and having access to the critical supplies contained within is essential. As more and more people choose to lose their ability to take care of themselves, the need to keep your supplies from the prying eyes of the desperately unprepared grows even more.

5. Assurance during uncertain times

Assurance during uncertain or difficult times is closely associated with the aforementioned creating surplus. Volatile stock market activity, economic recession/depression talk, the devaluation of the U.S. dollar, and overall condition of world affairs creates a negative tone of uncertainty within society. It is very difficult not to be influenced or consumed with the fear mongering that drives many people into panic mode. The old adage of "Better to have it and not need it, than to need it and not have it" is the prevailing thought among preppers.

Much like the squirrel, humans tend to stash away provisions for later use when those items are scarce or limited. Photo courtesy of www.pixabay.com.

6. Self-imposed rationing

There are times when people hide items merely to slow the eventual consumption of those items. Anyone who has children will know what I mean by this. As parents, we hide snack foods and candy, in an effort to keep the kids from eating an entire box of snack cakes or a whole bag of potato chips in one sitting.

While it is possible to delve deeper into some of the sociological and psychological reasons on an individual basis, the previous list provides a reasonable overview without belaboring the issue with multiple theories and conjecture. While I do not hold either type of these degrees, the criminology and deviant behavior courses I took in college do form the basis of my opinions on the subject.

While this photo is only a training scenario, how will the average citizen react or respond to their doors being forcibly kicked open by police, the National Guard, or marauders and looters? Photo courtesy of www.pixabay.com.

One may ask why I would choose to disclose all these types of diversion safes. Does it make it easier for criminals to hide drugs and contraband items? Maybe. Does it aid law enforcement who might overstep the bounds of a search warrant? Possibly. Does it make it harder for people to keep their valuables safe? Probably. These are not easy questions with simple, straightforward answers in many scenarios.

To take full advantage of the information presented in this book, one should approach the topic with an investigative mindset like Sir Arthur Conan Doyle's logical detective character, Sherlock Holmes. One should apply the use of inferences, deductive reasoning, and logic to locate and/or prevent the discovery of hidden valuables.

Most of us will not have this type of cash reserve available to us. The unreliability and unpredictability of financial markets and currency may render any cash surplus irrelevant. Photo courtesy of www.pixabay.com.

For example, if there is a can of Aqua Net hairspray in the home of a 75-year-old widower, how much hairspray does he actually use? Do his white, wispy side locks adequately disguise the surely inevitable signs of male pattern baldness? Are there any photos that can substantiate and justify his possession of hair spray? Probably not. Therefore, a can of hairspray would then be suspicious and worthy of closer inspection. In preparation for the chapters to come, I spent a significant amount of time surfing the internet, pinning posts on Pinterest, buying products, and researching the various types of diversion safes currently available. There are literally hundreds, possibly thousands more, that are hand-made, homemade, or ready-made to stash valuables.

While the intent of this book is to aid in the discovery and/or recovery of hidden stashes and caches, I realize the potential for the opposite, as well. Some will use the information to better develop hiding places or reduce liabilities by fortifying weaker caches and hiding places.

Depending on any prolonged duration of any SHTF event, supplies will eventually run out. In addition, not every well-prepared prepper and self-proclaimed survivalist will, if fact, survive. Circumstances beyond anyone's control can take out even the most prepared individual.

Here is a hypothetical situation: A man has been prepping for several years and has ample supplies in reserve to see that his wife and his two young children will have the basics that they need for a nine months. However, the timing of the event strikes during rush hour traffic and the EMP halts freeway traffic with stalled vehicles and multiple collisions. His family is killed in one of the resulting collisions. Even worse, they slowly die, as it is impossible for rescue workers to respond to the sheer number of casualties. Communications are non-existent, despite the emergency kit in the trunk that included a communications device sealed in a small faraday cage. He waits for three days, with no communications, no news, and with dwindling hope. After two weeks, his grief gets the better of him or is more than he can emotionally tolerate and he commits suicide.

I'm telling you, the psychological and emotional trauma produced by events such as these on a large scale will send many people over the edge. You will most likely see both tremendous feats of human resilience and desperation, along with those once thought to have resiliency and courage crumble to the ground in absolute panic and terror.

To be honest, I don't know if I would survive or would even want to under certain conditions. So, I don't even try to put myself on a pedestal declaring that I'd be impervious to the myriad of "what ifs" that could instantly manifest in any particular SHTF scenario.

In order to justify my reasoning for the inclusion of both how to hide and how to locate caches and stashed supplies, I simply regard it as my contribution to those who have both chosen to prepare in advance and those who find this book by chance or by necessity. There is no doubt the world will get uglier and more uncertain should a massive SHTF event take place. All I can ever hope is that the people who find this book and read it, find it valuable to them as they attempt to survive the unknown future.

Citations:

1. https://leb.fbi.gov/2012/april/focus-on-searches-characteristics -and-implications-of-diversion-safes

2. https://www.usatoday.com/story/news/politics/2017/12/29/state-releases-huma-abedins-work-docs-found-anthony-weiners-computer/990912001/

Chapter 2:
Diversion Safe Pitfalls and How to Detect Them

Diversion safes thrive upon the multitudes of food and beverage choices available to disguise it among other legitimate food items. Opportunistic intruders are far less likely to take large amounts of time rummaging through an entire pantry of canned goods to find your secret stash.

While this is the primary advantage against the burglars, law enforcement and/or government agents generally take their time inspecting every single item that holds the potential of storing evidence or contraband during the execution of a search warrant. Because of this fact, certain disadvantages become glaringly apparent within the edibles/consumables group.

1. The Expiration Date Pitfall

Almost every consumable food item, whether it be canned, jarred, bagged or boxed has an expiration or 'best if used by' date. While some will argue the validity of the expiration date, protesting that as long as the can is not dented, bulging, or leaking and the contents pass the sniff test, it is edible. Whether the reader agrees with that theory is a matter of personal choice and conviction.

Expiration dates stamped on canned goods can expose a diversion safe very easily.
Photo courtesy of pixabay.com.

A can with a past expiration date has the potential of catching the attention of the well-intentioned housewife and is promptly disposed of in the trash. New Years diets, and excuses like, "Nobody eats this stuff, anyway" also lead to the accidental discarding of a diversion safe. In the trash, means good-bye stash, so choose your diversion safe wisely. You don't want it to be so rare to your palette that you have to convince others that you enjoy the container's contents. Likewise, you also don't want it to be your favorite pantry item, either.

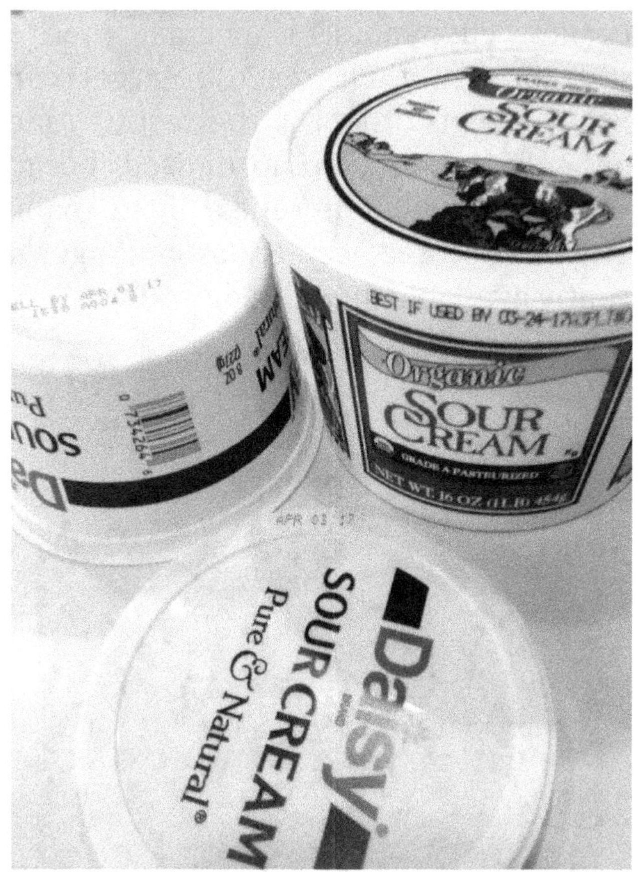

Some containers have expiration dates on both the lid and on the bottom of the container. Others may have the date on the lid edge. Photo by author.

If you're proactive enough and have a good memory, on some containers like the previous sour cream photo, you can swap out a new lid after you use the contents. This, of course, depends upon your allegiance to a particular brand to ensure the correct lid size.

2. The New Look-Same Great Taste Pitfall

In order to stay relevant in the economy, companies must market and advertise their product to entice new customers or to make their product more appealing to their desired target consumer. This often means that a perfectly functioning diversion safe is now compromised because the product packaging that it relies on to maintain its anonymity has become obsolete or no longer matches the currently available/marketed product.

This can design hasn't been in production for years. This is an example of the dilemma you may face when manufacturer's redesign their product labels with a new look to influence customers to purchase their product. Photo by author.

Most major brands will change packaging every 5-10 years, however, iconic brands like Coca-Cola rarely stray from their famous trademark.

Soda cans are highly susceptible to packaging changes, putting them at greater risk of discovery. Photo courtesy of www.pixabay.com.

3. The Use It and Lose It Pitfall

This situation inadvertently happens when other family members or guests don't know where you are hiding your private slush fund, valuables, or other "for your eyes only" type stuff. You are rushing to prepare dinner and send a family member to retrieve a can of soup from the pantry, they return soup in hand, and you start opening the can with the can opener, and destroy the safe. In addition, now everyone around is now interested or curious as to what you were hiding. Busted.

Here is another example; your drinking buddy comes over to watch the game. You tell him the brewskys are in the fridge, and he selects the lone can of Heineken shoved in the back. He plops down on the couch and cracks open a can containing no beer. He's mad because you teased him with the temptation of his favorite import and you're mad because he figuratively poured $15 worth of imported deception down the drain.

4. If It Rattles, It Tattles Pitfall

One thing many forget to do is pad the interior storage area to keep metallic valuables from moving around inside. You must consider the potential of losing over half of the interior storage space to adequate padding to keep contents from making any noise should someone pick up the safe and give it a good shake.   Diversion safes that portray liquid contents on the outer packaging are harder to convincingly disguise.

5. It Betrays What It Weighs Pitfall

As if rattling contents weren't bad enough, it's harder hiding items that weigh more than the net weight of the contents listed on the label. Most commercial diversion safes contain a weighted filler to fool the casual observer into believing the contents are genuine when handled. For example, a can of soda contains 12 fluid ounces. If you try to hide a 100 Nosler .30 caliber 125-grain ballistic-tip bullets in a pop can, it's going to weigh more than 12 ounces. It's not always a matter of whether or not the safe will hold the contents, but rather if the contents will create a tell demanding further examination.

6. The Ghost Resident Pitfall

The ghost resident is the person (or animal) who does not physically live in the dwelling but somehow manages to have evidence of the contrary. Households without dogs should not have a dog food diversion safe. Nor should a bachelor use a tampon box to hide cash in the bathroom. Likewise, a woman who has a carburetor cleaner diversion safe and doesn't know what a carburetor is or that her fuel-injected car doesn't have one is going to be suspicious as well.

This is not to disparage or exalt either sex, but to point out how someone deploying deductive reasoning and logic can pick apart and discover a hide location.

7. The Internet Pitfall

While the Internet is a great resource tool to discovering diversion safes and learning of their construction and concealment methods, it also suffers as the fruit from the forbidden tree. Once the knowledge is exposed, it is now available to whoever chooses to use it, regardless of the manner in which they intend to use the knowledge.

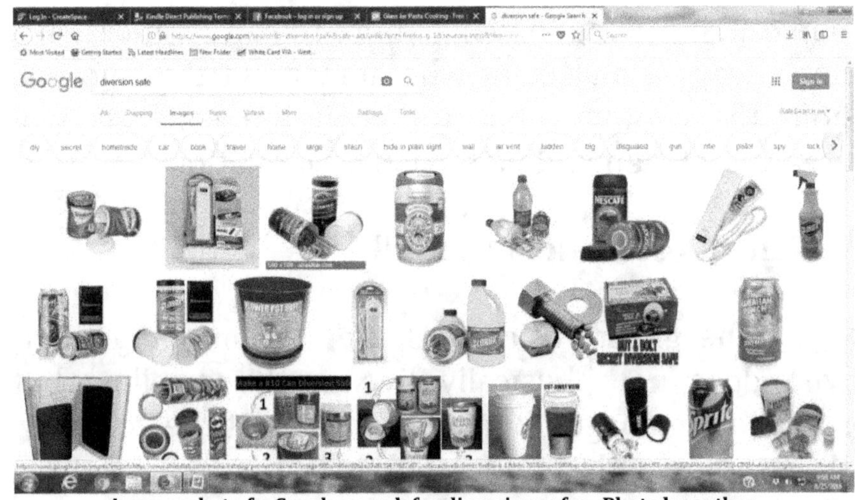

A screenshot of a Google search for diversion safes. Photo by author.

8. The Repetition of Repeated Redundancy Pitfall

One can tell by the heading what the pitfall describes. Having more than one diversion safe has some merit. However, too many or of the same type of diversion safe opens the door to having your belongings taken, especially if someone catches a lucky break and discovers the initial one.

These pitfalls also serve as evidential clues to discover hidden stashes left behind by other people. There have been countless stories of people who have purchased a home and found money tucked away in some tiny, forgotten nook. Most often, people find sentimental keepsakes and memorabilia collections rather than something having any vast monetary value. However, coin collections usually turn up a couple of valuable pieces and occasionally, some substantial cash reserves are found.

Chapter 3:
Diversion Safes Disguised as Edible Consumables

One of the great contributions of the commercially available diversions safe is its ability to inspire the creation of homemade diversion safes. Oftentimes this occurs for a couple of reasons. First, commercial diversion safes vary in price from very affordable to legally swindling you out of your hard-earned money. Second, because the commercial variety is widely available without restriction, some purchasers feel that their "popularity" diminishes their intended effectiveness.

I'll start by categorizing commercial diversion safes into two basic, broad categories. This chapter will focus on the edible consumables, with Chapter 4 highlighting the non-edible consumables. It is possible for any homemade diversion safe to qualify for both categories. However, if one were going to put forth the time and effort to make their own diversion safe, they should carefully avoid some of the detection pitfalls associated with the more common commercial varieties.

With a little ingenuity, patience, and planning, you can create your own realistic looking diversion safes without having to watch countless hours of Martha Stewart home decor/crafting shows or YouTube videos. The point is to select a container capable of storing the intended valuable(s).

Keep in mind, a majority of all the commercially available diversion safes listed and featured throughout this book are almost exclusively American-made products. The availability of these products in other countries may be extremely limited or considered prohibited or restricted.

COMMON EDIBLE/CONSUMABLE DIVERSION SAFES

Aluminum Cans - Aluminum can diversion safes are among the most popular and widely available. While there are several sodas and beer varieties, only some of the most popular brands/flavors exist in the realm of diversion safes. Pay particular attention to canned teas, coffee beverages, and energy drinks. All of the below listed brands have a commercially available or pictured diversion safe on the Internet. Be sure to thoroughly check and inspect the following brands:

Soda and Soft Drink Cans

Diversion safes come in several varieties of popular soda brands, making it sometimes difficult to tell the difference. Photo courtesy of www.pixabay.com.

Coca-Cola
Diet Coke
Sprite
Hawaiian Punch
RC Cola
Diet Rite
Dr. Pepper
7-Up
Cherry 7-Up
A & W Root Beer
Mountain Dew
Country Time Strawberry Lemonade
Canada Dry Ginger Ale
Brisk Iced Tea

Arizona Iced Tea
Arizona Lemonade
Arizona Green Tea
V8 Vegetable Juice

Beers and Malt Liquor Cans

Budweiser
Bud Light
Corona Extra
Tecate
Coors
Coors Light
Miller Lite
Miller High Life
Miller Genuine Draft
Stroh's Light
Pabst Blue Ribbon
Heineken
Modelo
Carlton Draught
Schlitz Malt Liquor
Olde English "800" Malt Liquor
Old Milwaukee
Hamm's
Olympia

Energy Drinks and Bottled Water

Red Bull
Monster
Nōs

Rock Star
Starbuck's Doubleshot Energy
Starbuck's Refreshers
Aquafina
Dasanti

Can you tell which can is the diversion safe just by looking at it? That's why diversion safes work so well. Photo courtesy of www.pixabay.com.

Metal/Steel Cans - Steel cans contain anything from fruits and vegetables to dog food.

Campbell's Chunky Soup
Maxwell House Coffee
Del Monte Fruit Cocktail
Del Monte Sliced Peaches
Del Monte Mixed Vegetables
SW Texas-Style BBQ Beans
Van Camps Pork and Beans
Libby's Jumbo-Can Cut Green Beans

Campbell's Condensed Chicken Noodle Soup
Hunt's Pasta Sauce
Heinz Vegetarian Beans
Campbell's Spaghetti O's
Chef Boyardee Beefaroni
PAM Cooking Spray
Reddi-Whip

Diversion safes featuring foreign food products have the potential to be either an asset or a liability for storing hidden items. Photo courtesy of www.pixabay.com.

Plastic Containers - As plastic containers are not subject to rust and take considerable time to break down environmentally, they make great storage devices. However, they can melt when exposed to direct heat/sunlight and chemical byproducts from the plastic can potentially leach into the container contents.

Nescafe Instant Coffee
Old-Fashioned Peanut Butter
JIF Peanut Butter
Best Foods Real Mayonnaise
Kraft Mayo
Miracle-Whip
Minute Maid Frozen Juice Concentrate
Pepcid Complete
Centrum Silver Multi-vitamins
Mini Oreo Go-Packs
Nutter Butter Bites Go-Packs
Teddy Grahams Go-Packs
Mentos Gum
Coffee-Mate Creamer
Bailey's coffee Creamer

Capped Paper Tubes

These types of food containers are often repurposed for storing non-food items. We used to use Pringles cans to sort and store spent brass, which would later be reloaded into ammunition. Photo courtesy of www.pixabay.com.

Pringles Potato Crisps
Tootsie Roll Safes
Morton Salt
Swiss Miss Hot Cocoa
Star Snacks Roasted Peanuts
Trader Joe's Sea Salt

This is just a sampling of the types of products that have a commercially available diversion safe version of their product. There are thousands upon thousands of other food and beverage products that can be used or modified with little effort into a functional and discreet diversion safe.

Small containers such as this mint container can be repurposed to hold cash, flash drives, or anything else that fits within the interior dimensions. Photo by author.

Another factor to consider is that some food containers, like mayonnaise, for example, have a smell. Hiding items in a smaller, insertable container and then placing it into a mayonnaise jar may seem like a good tactic, but be prepared to change out the host jar when the product expires.

To add to the already large amount of potential diversion safes, when you include the reusing/repurposing of other common containers such as metal tins once containing mints or lozenges, the possibilities become endless.

Chapter 4:
Diversion Safes Disguised as Non-Edible Consumables

The inedible consumables category of diversion safes are plagued by most of the same pitfalls as their previously listed cousins. The only marked difference is that most, if not all, of the products do not have an expiration date.   Toilet bowl cleaner bought and stored years ago will probably be just as effective as toilet bowl cleaner bought today. This is not to say the product reliability cannot degrade over time, but the likelihood of a diversion safe being discovered because of a well-expired "Best if used by" date is greatly reduced.

With that said, the non-edible consumable diversion safes are still subject to the other pitfalls listed back in Chapter Two.

Personal Hygiene and Grooming Products - As a society, we Americans are tremendously vain when it comes to personal hygiene and cleanliness.   This almost fanatical obsession to control or eliminate all traces of body odor has produced a variety of grooming products that have found a secondary market in the realm of diversion safes. The commercially available safes are listed below:

Hygiene Items

Brut Deodorant
Barbasol Shaving Cream
Axe Body Spray
Aqua Net Hairspray
Aussie Travel-Size Hairspray
Gillette Foamy Shaving Cream
XtraCare Shave Cream
Desenex Foot Spray
Edge Shave Gel
Suave Hairspray
Barbasol Pure Silk Shave Cream
Speed Stick Deodorant
Cruex Antifungal Spray

Personal Care Items

Hairbrushes
Lint Rollers
Chap-Stick
Lipstick

Clothing

Cocktail Dresses
Shirts

Jackets
Suits
Underwear
Shoes

There are diversion safes manufactured to look like shirts and dresses. Any garment with pockets has the potential to hide something of value. Photo courtesy of www.pixabay.com.

Pet Food

Pedigree Dog Food
Kibbles N' Bits Dog Food

Pesticides

Black Flag Roach Spray

Paints and Preservatives

Black Bear Paints Company
LusterCare Rust Preventative Coating

Automotive Care

Super-X Tire Inflator
Tite-Seal
STP Son-of-a-Gun Tire Cleaner
Liquid Wrench
Gunk Engine Degreaser
Gunk Big Puncture Seal
Gunk Motor Flush
Johnson's Brake Parts Cleaner
Armor-All Cleaning Wipes
Armor-All Glass Wipes
WD-40
JB Oil Treatment
JB Fuel Injector System Cleaner

Household Cleaners

Power-House All-Purpose Cleaner
Power-House Oven Cleaner
Power-House Bathroom Cleaner
Power-House Fabric & Upholstery Cleaner
Lysol Disinfectant Spray
Ajax Powder Cleanser
Comet Powder Cleanser
Ultra Duster
Love My Carpet

Carpet Fresh
Air Wick
Scotch Gard Carpet Protector
Scotch-Brite Stainless Steel Cleaner/Polish
Clorox Wipes
Clorox Bleach
Smith & Wesson Bore & Action Cleaner

Other Hiding Places

Briefcases
Attaché cases
Airline Luggage
Plastic Storage Bins
Moving Boxes

The amount of time needed to search everything pictured here thoroughly is deterrent enough for most opportunistic criminals and petty thieves. The longer they stay, the greater the chances of their discovery and possible arrest. Photo courtesy of www.pixabay.com.

These lists are far from exhaustive or complete. Most of the items listed were items I found searching the Internet with the key word search "diversion safe."

Chapter 5:
Home Decor Diversion Safes

A house is not a home unless it has the cozy feel attributed to the inclusion of furnishings and keepsakes. Framed pictures of family and loved ones, accent pillows, and knick-knacks are all items one expects to be present in a home.

Probably the most popular of all diversion safes is a longtime classic: the hollowed-out book. Centuries ago, only the rich and well-educated had books. Books themselves were expensive to print, so of course, only rich people owned them. Rich people, therefore, had money and valuables; and those items needed to be safeguarded. Since many people were also illiterate, books would most likely not be an enticement for would-be thieves to search.

Some of these items appear rather fake and so great caution should be exercised when choosing these as a potential diversion safe. Others are disguised so well, that the potential of forgetting about them is also a reality to consider.

Clock safes often require batteries to operate and seasonal time adjustments. Sometimes the clock mechanisms are not good quality and the clock will not keep accurate time. Furthermore, they do not provide the most secure hiding option for certain items. There is no locking mechanism to protect valuables and can be forcibly removed from the wall unless additional reinforcement is added. Photo by author.

Household Items

Compact Disc (CD) Cases
Batteries
Sugar Dispensers
Wall Outlets
Duct Covers
Flower Pots
Books
Mantle Clocks
Wall Clocks
Candles
Marks-A-Lot Permanent Markers
Stainless Steel Spray Bottles
BIC Cigarette Lighters
Closet Lights

Playing Cards
Nuts & Bolts
8-Ball Keychain
Toilet Paper Dispenser Spindles
Travel Mugs
Outdoor Sprinkler Heads
Thermometers
Surge Protectors
Chair Cushions
Throw Pillows
Floating Wall Shelves

Cigarette lighters, while quite small, can hold flash drives, currency, or drugs. Photo courtesy of www.pixabay.com.

Certain items require regular maintenance to ensure it functions correctly as a decoy, particularly clocks or other items operating on batteries or items that may need routine cleaning. Other items may be discovered when they do not operate according to their characteristics like batteries, sprinkler heads, wall outlets, and surge protectors. For this reason, some of these types of diversion safes are at high risk of accidental disposal when they appear not to work.

Other items such as throw pillows often gets overlooked, as people often assume the only thing within the pillow is the polyester stuffing. It would be quite easy to place five $100 bills inside and never change the weight of the pillow.

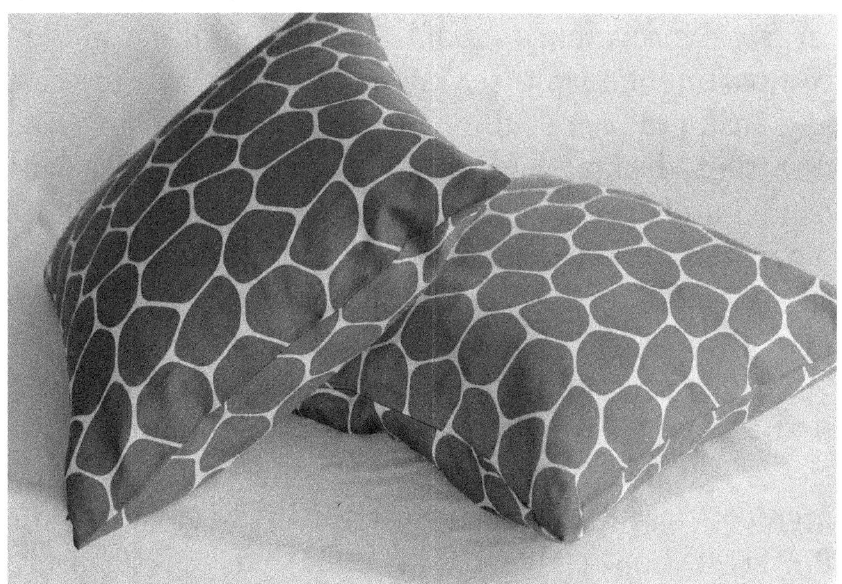

Despite the stereotypical male distain for accent pillows, they make a great hiding place for items weighing less than one or two ounces. Photo courtesy of www.pixabay.com.

Chapter 6:
Furniture Diversion Safes

During the last several years, there has been a larger prevalence of custom-built hidden compartment furniture. Websites such as Pinterest and Instagram are full of photographs of customized furniture designed for hiding all types of firearms from handguns to large-caliber rifles. The AR-15, when completely disassembled, can fit into places too small to hide the fully assembled weapon.

I'm probably more obsessed with this subject than I ought, but I'm fascinated by the some of the clever designs available and the craftsmanship involved creating these safes. I have a whole Pinterest board filled with hundreds of furniture designs featuring hidden compartments.

Probably the greatest cause for the rise in popularity of such furniture designs is the growing political uncertainty in the United States. This is coupled with the overall feelings of government mistrust and both the blatant and secretive attacks on individual freedoms perpetrated by our elected representatives and appointed officials alike.

What this has done, however, has bolstered entrepreneurship within the American economy. It has also created a market for American-made handcrafted furniture again. Both are positive growth indicators for the economy.

This corner hutch features handcrafted quality and very unassuming design making it capable of storing all sorts of valuables inside while still functioning as a display case for china or other knickknacks. Photo by New Jersey Concealment Furniture, Used with permission.

It should be easily recognizable that smaller firearms are much easier to hide and conceal than larger ones. Because of this, it's not always necessary or feasible to have a larger piece of furniture to conceal a small handgun and a couple of spare magazines. However, there are furniture makers who specialize in larger pieces designed to conceal larger rifles.

This unassuming coat rack and shelf offers secret storage and rapid accessibility to its contents. Photo by New Jersey Concealment Furniture. Used with permission.

This also includes ideas such as placing weighted, waterproof containers in toilet tanks, false plumbing, false HVAC (Heating, Ventilation, and Air-Conditioning) ductwork, false walls, and access points/crawlspaces. There are more highly detailed books available for some of these types of projects. A list of these books is included in the reference section of this book.

The increased popularity with any of these types of concealment furniture pieces means people will begin to search for them. They can sometimes lack adequate locking mechanisms, as they rely on their appearance of something incapable of hidden storage, rather than having a high security rating in terms of locks.

The most common locking mechanism is a spring-loaded plunger-type rod that is opened with a magnet. Hypothetically, someone armed with a pry bar and a magnet could make short work of one of these safes, where alternatively criminals or scavengers would have to spend hours drilling a safe in order to gain access to the contents.

However, proper OPSEC practices are mentioned in my book, *Conversational Camouflage.* Those concepts will help remind readers about what they say and who they speak to when discussing hide locations.

Chapter 7:
Hidden Rooms

Like most American boys growing up in the 70s, I watched the old Batman television series starring Adam West and Burt Ward. I think it was almost every boy's dream to have a secret lair or hidden room. Today, these rooms are no longer just the stuff of television or the exclusive ownership of the rich, well-to-do members of society.

As a child, I wanted a bookcase that secretly opened and revealed a hidden passageway. These types of doors are still commercially available. Photo courtesy of www.pixabay.com.

Hidden rooms are difficult to construct unless you have better than average carpentry skills. My father converted a small storage room in the basement of the house we lived in when I was a teenager. The outer wall had good quality wood paneling and the entrance door lined up with the grooves in the paneling. A magnetic plunger was used to pop the door open when you pushed on the door panel. This was our gunroom, where we kept the gun safes, ammunition, and reloading equipment out of sight. Unless you knew it was there, it looked like just a regular paneled wall.

On an adjacent wall, the ducting for the HVAC systems required us to frame around it and cover it with drywall. I used the void created at one end to stash toilet paper and computer disks with "target" information secretly for future TPing adventures with my friends. In the years we lived at that house, my stash was never discovered by anyone I deemed as "unauthorized".

There are often some obvious tells or at least some things that will raise suspicions regarding the existence of a secret room or passageway.

Leads to Nowhere Plumbing - Some of the more amateur efforts will have plumbing or electrical conduit running into a seemingly solid wall for no apparent reason.

Drafts - Cracks and crevices are notorious for producing drafts, especially in older homes. However, drafts are also notorious for revealing secret passageways, voids, and storage areas. They are most often detected when the HVAC systems turn on and there is sufficient force from the unit to push air from any ducting in the hidden area out into other portions of the structure.

Full Length Bookshelves - Any room in a house featuring a full-length, corner-to-corner bookshelf will raise suspicions; at least mine, anyway. Furthermore, any bookcase or nook that looks like it is or was at one time, a doorway is worthy of further inspection.

Gaps exposing interior light - Oftentimes, a big mistake exposing the detection of a hidden room is light escaping from the room. It's important to remember to seal or block gaps and cracks where light can escape. It's also helpful to install lighting that operates on timers or a motion sensor. They can be set to turn off the lighting, should you forget to flick the wall switch.

Fortunately, well designed (and less discussed publicly) hidden rooms are difficult to detect. In some cases, significant technological resources such as ground-penetrating radar, thermal sensors, and structure scanners must be used to locate hidden rooms. Usually, only the police or government agencies have this type of equipment and they can only use it in conjunction with a warrant to search.

Chapter 8:
Outdoor Caches

Outdoor caches are very popular because of the great multitude of potential hiding places. Because caches still may be discovered during the execution of a search warrant, most people avoid hiding an outdoor cache of any major contraband on their property. There are three main cache types typically used in outdoor covert storage. They are burial caches, aerial caches, and ground level caches.

Burial Caches

Burial caches are among the most popular stockpiling methods for contraband items, especially firearms. Every election cycle that produces a Democrat winner in the White House, reinitiates the discussion of caches at gun shows, online forums, and social media groups. While any type of storage container can be used, the PVC improvised burial tube is now commonplace. There are a couple of reasons for this. First, the material itself is water-proof (necessary for its original plumbing use) and second, it resists corrosion and decomposition.

Larger burial caches have their place and are better suited for your final bug-out destination. Until you arrive at your final bug-out location, you may not want or be able to carry all of the gear you originally put in a large en route cache. There are alternatives to large and buried caches. These will be discussed later in the chapter, but I wanted to lay the groundwork to argue the rationale of using those methods over the more traditional burial cache.

While the best justification of burial caches is the old adage of "Out of sight, out of mind" and that marauders cannot raid what they cannot find or see, there are disadvantages that need addressing. I am not a fan of large burial tubes, although they may be necessary for larger gear and supplies.

Two such alternatives are aerial concealment and exposed/ground level concealment. The key word to remember here is *practical*. The type of cache you decide to use depends on some important factors based upon your age, your physical condition, and your environment. Here are some points to consider in selecting your cache method.

1. What kind of equipment do you need to hide or retrieve the cache? A spade equates to digging. Digging equates to work. Work expends needed calories and energy. Even with a perfect hide location, digging requires the disposal of the excess soil to make the surrounding area look undisturbed. This is especially true if there is a chance of someone walking through your proposed cache site. With all the effort put in to bury the cache in the dirt, you inevitably end up removing the dirt again to get to your supplies.

2. Time is not always on your side. Just as digging equates to work, work equates to time. When the time comes to retrieve the tube, are you really going to want to spend the time digging for items when you could be having a jumpstart to your bug-out location? Will you have enough time to sit around and wait for the cover of darkness or ideal weather conditions to retrieve your cache? Carrying an adequate spade or shovel to your hide location is going to look somewhat suspicious. If you are planning to use an easier concealed camp shovel to unearth your treasure, then you are adding even more time to the retrieval process. What if someone follows you, waiting until you are distracted or exhausted from the retrieval process, and decides to attack or arrest you?

This could also happen in other cache retrieval methods, but your situational awareness is not going to be at its peak if you are concentrating on digging. Certain cache types require more vigilance because your attention is divided between the retrieval process and maintaining situational awareness. Too much time spent in an area, no matter how secure you deem it to be, can put you at risk for discovery. In a SERE scenario, stopping to hide or retrieve something in the ground is going to use up time that needs to be spent putting distance between you and your pursuers.

3.   Mother Nature will not cooperate during a SHTF event. Regardless of whatever causes a SHTF event requiring a bug-out to a more secure location, Mother Nature and *Murphy's Law* will persist in their usual defiance of human endeavors and success. If things can go wrong, they will; and they will do so at the most inconvenient time and season. Inclement weather is one thing, but combine the first two reasons with the addition of snow and several inches of frozen ground and you have now increased the amount of time and hard digging required. Moreover, freezing conditions can reduce manual dexterity, adding more time digging or climbing and exposes your body to the elements for longer periods.

4. Some cache methods and sizes may require an accomplice. Trust is a big factor when you start obligating friends to swear an oath of secrecy. The old expression, "Two can keep a secret if one is dead," is something to keep in mind. Anyone who knows or associates with you who encounters unfriendly forces are a potential risk for compromise. These forces threaten or intimidate people into turning on you and revealing your secrets.

Having a cache location that only you know about and only you can access/retrieve your goods without assistance is the safest policy. If one man walks into the woods with a shovel or rope looks suspicious, then two or more men with shovels and ropes screams of a conspiracy.

5. Larger caches are difficult to hide. If you choose to have a larger cache site, you run the greater risk of its discovery. The best advice I can give is to resist the temptation to store all your essential supplies in a single large cache. Making several, smaller caches along your travel route are wiser choices. First, your cache locations are more scattered and random. Second, if one cache is raided, discovered, or destroyed, you only lose some assets instead of all of them. An event such as this is frustrating, but you continue on to your next location, knowing that you did not lose everything.

6. How remote is the cache location? Location and remoteness also determine what type of cache is best for your situation. The more traffic, whether human or animal, will require more effort to conceal it. The more difficult it is to reach your cache in terms of remoteness and terrain, the better your chances will be keeping it hidden. While you want to make it difficult for everyone else to discover and reach, you do not want to put yourself in peril in order to conceal or retrieve your cache.

Since there are already several books written about underground and burial caches available, I would recommend that you purchase those books. There is no need for me to re-hash the information presently available.

So what are the alternatives? There are a few concealment options, and like burial tubes, they are not without their own unique drawbacks. However, these cache options eliminate or reduce some of the labor drawbacks associated with burial tubes. When the full use of technology and camouflaging techniques are applied, the appeal of the alternatives will overcome most of the negative aspects. It is important to understand that there are no 100% foolproof methods to conceal caches.

Aerial Caches

I often tell people to consider the use of aerial caches over traditional buried caches. When discussing aerial concealment, it is important to realize that you do not want your cache swinging from branches. The first option is suspending the tube within the canopy of a deciduous tree giving you the ability to retrieve the tube by lowering with an attached rope. The option of nestling the tube in one of the higher crotches of the tree is the best. The most important thing to remember with an 'aerial' tube is to secure it tightly so that it cannot be dislodged by high winds or strike other portions of the tree and thereby bringing attention to it.

Humans are not tree climbers by nature. Without some sort of assistance like ropes or ladders, the desire and ability to climb trees decreases with age for most people. For some people, climbing a tree to retrieve a cache can be unsafe and potentially dangerous. Climbing trees in cold weather can be difficult. If attempts are made while wearing gloves or mittens, the success rate usually drops while the inherent dangers and risks increase. Therefore, most individuals do not give tree canopies a second thought while looking for hidden objects. The only time a person's attention is drawn to the tree canopy is when the sun reflects off an object or noises such as clanging, rubbing, or creaking alert someone of an object hidden within the canopy.

An aerial cache suspended within an aspen grove would be difficult to detect visually.
Photo courtesy of www.pixabay.com.

Aerial caches are not subject to some of the technology used to aid in the detection of buried caches. If any searching agency has any inkling that you have buried items on your property, they quickly dispatch metal detectors, ground-penetrating radar, and seismic equipment to detect whether the ground has been disturbed. This is not to say those technologies cannot be foiled, but many officials are well aware of the methods used to create false positives. Experienced searchers also do not stop at the first uncovered piece of metal they dig up. They continue digging to be sure nothing is left undiscovered.

Small aerial caches like this one can be hoisted and secured into tall trees and remain relatively unnoticed, especially in remote locations. Photo by author.

The other advantage of the aerial cache is they eliminate the need for elaborate decoys or the creation of false positives for detection equipment. This saves a lot of time and effort. In regions where bear and other large predatory animals are present, aerial caches can keep your supplies from being raided.

All caches need to be properly sealed in order to keep water and pests from entering in and damaging the cache contents. Photo by author.

There are some obvious characteristics that need consideration, as far as tree selection is concerned. You should have an idea of what the tree looks like with its full summer canopy and during its winter dormancy. Cache detection is greater during the winter months, as the foliage of the canopy can no longer camouflage the cache after the leaves fall.

Ground Level Caches

For ease of access, nothing can beat a ground level cache.   However, the level of concealment needed for this method is quite high.   The effort required to conceal them properly and the high risk for discovery of hidden items usually frightens people from using ground level caches. However, for items in which you may need faster access to, a ground level cache may be of benefit to you or your group.

This concept is more prevalent with the popularity of geocaching.   Geo-caches are small, manmade objects hidden within a natural setting. They contain little log books to record who finds the object and when.   Because of this is the direct opposite of what you want to accomplish, the camouflage MUST be exceptional for your cache to remain hidden. With some ingenuity and creativity, this is easily accomplished.

Incidentally, with these methods, you are not restricted to tubes. Food-grade five-gallon buckets with gamma seal lids hidden under rock piles, large tree stumps, etc. also work well. Large fake rocks made of plastic often used to disguise well housings and residential utilities work well as concealment, too.   However, I strongly recommend adding additional textured spray paint along with gluing preserved moss on the surface to give the appearance of realism.

Buried cable/utility posts can be purchased and used as a small supply cache enroute to a bug out location (BOL). They look official and like they belong when placed properly, with a low likelihood of disturbance. Photo courtesy of Jake Lang. Used with permission.

There are two very important things to remember with ground concealment techniques. First, the object you use must look like it belongs in that location and second, it should look like it has been there for years. There is a certain level of creative artistry that must be administered to this concealment technique. As you would want to choose a location to have the least amount of human contact or presence, you still need to be prepared for both accidental and intentional detection. Take advantage of all the natural camouflage and concealment available in your proposed cache location.

Metal utility boxes can also be used, but they are much more susceptible to corrosion over time. Photo courtesy of Jake Lang. Used with permission.

Distressing and gouging the surface of a PVC pipe with an air sander can create the illusion of a weathered log. The author used 60 grit sandpaper to scuff the surface. This process also removed the semi-glossy sheen of new PVC pipe and gave it a wood grain appearance. Photo by author.

The previous three pictures feature the progression of a small PVC pipe cache I once made for hiding along my route to a bug-out location in the event of an urban disaster that prevented me from bugging in. They had to be small enough to carry in a backpack, yet large enough to hold some essential supplies, food, and water. Finalized steps included the use of a Dremel tool to cut grooves mimicking the paths created by wood boring insects and gluing patches of bark from other fallen timber to certain portions of the tube. Another method to reduce the perfect, man-made shape is to gently warm the tube enough to distort the exterior without melting or burning the PVC.

As a teenager, I concealed a gallon jug filled with water and dead grass. The fermentation of this mixture smelled horrible. In my typical teenage mischievousness, my friends and I would spray the liquid on people's porches or try to inject it through window screens. Now, a white jug shoved in a stack of brown and gray colored wood sticks out like a cockroach on bread. Some portions of the pile were covered with a tarp. Later, I ended up spray-painting the exposed portions of the jug to camouflage it better.

Natural Caches

Some of the most tempting cache locations are the ones you find out in nature. Caves have long been used as cache and plunder hideouts from prehistoric times through the time of pirates and marauders. Despite their tempting ready-to-use look, some of these natural alcoves are not suited for long term storage of goods and supplies. Cave exploration can be fun and adventuresome when conducted with proper training and correct gear. However, caves often contain many hazards and risks that should be assessed thoroughly before using them as potential cache locations.

Despite the temptation to store provisions or make a natural cache, caves are a source of curiosity to whomever or whatever happens to find it. Photo courtesy of www.pixabay.com.

Old tree stumps and fallen trees can also have the potential for cache use. Fallen timber is usually covered in both microscopic and visible organisms that will migrate toward your cache supplies, no matter how bug-proof, waterproof, and rot-proof you try to make it. I have also heard of people using abandoned animal dens as caches, but this doesn't sound like the wisest choice, either.

You also need to ensure and implement the best waterproofing methods you have at your disposal, as surface hides are much more susceptible to water seepage. Sealing every possible point where water can seep into your cache with a silicone sealant is a prudent decision. Even if your cache never is exposed to direct rainfall, dew and condensation can still creep into unsealed caches. As an added measure, make sure to use desiccant packs to absorb any moisture.

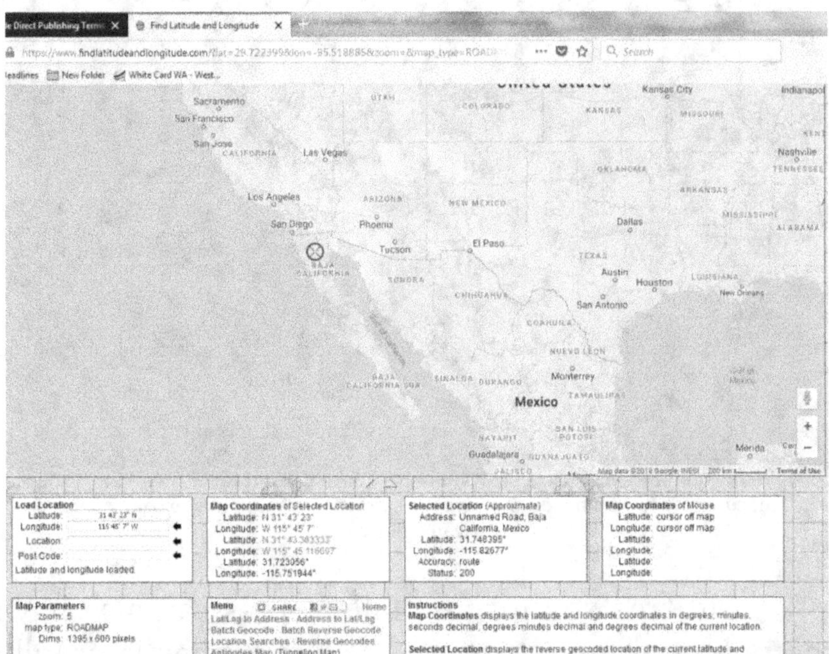

There are plenty of websites providing coordinates. These can both be a blessing or a curse, so use caution when recording GPS coordinates. Screenshot photo by author.

The most important thing concerning personal caches is keep your mouth shut. This should go without mention, but you should never discuss the location of any cache you have or the types of products you use for your diversion safes. Social media is a wonderful place to search for new ideas and discover likeminded people. However, the people you engage with through the various social media outlets like Facebook, Pinterest, or Instagram, should not be considered trustworthy. Cache culture and concepts are usually safe to discuss, but never your exact cache coordinates or contents.

Second, if you move, don't forget to take it with you. Many people will offer the advice that you shouldn't write down the locations of your caches and they are right. However, that means you must proactively take steps to remember where you place your items.

If you choose to write down coordinates, try switching the latitude and longitude, switch compass points, or write the numbers backwards. These methods are obviously not foolproof, but would make it harder for someone to figure out where you've buried or placed your cache.

For example, if I bury a cache in the back property where I live in Australia, by switching to the opposite compass points respectively, the new location ends up in Baja, California. This method obviously won't work if the coordinates place you in any of the oceans, but it may confuse some people.

You should avoid using certain Smartphone apps like those used for recreational geocaching, as the whole purpose is to keep people from deliberately searching and discovering your cache.

Chapter 9:
Post-Apocalyptic Scavenging and Foraging

The main purpose of this chapter is to aid the urban survivalist in obtaining essential items in which he can either sell or barter in order to procure other necessary resources. In a post-apocalyptic world or in ravaged cities under martial law, this type of activity should be regarded as very dangerous. One must carefully consider the benefit to risk ratio, as there will be other like-minded individuals looking for the same opportunity to increase their survival chances.

In all other circumstances, it is illegal to force entry into dwellings for the express purpose of acquiring goods or property belonging to another person. However, when survival solely rests on basic food, water, shelter, and medical supplies, scavenging will become a reluctant, but all too necessary, activity at some point. Despite this perceived necessity, I still highly recommend that extreme caution be used and still advise against this practice if at all possible.

Abandoned property is just that, abandoned. The previous owner waives any claim or privacy regarding anything found in or on the property. Property abandonments are often subject to legally defined and specified time spans, but if the property has been abandoned in this type of scenario, the owner has either left or is deceased.

The unfortunate reality is in a true SHTF or TEOTWAWKI event, many people will die. No one can know for certain the numbers of casualties or how survivors will cope with the immense interruption to what we have come to know as normal life. The psychological and emotional trauma will be unlike anything we will possibly ever be able to quantify. Loss of life will range from hundreds to thousands and possibly millions, depending on the location of the disaster event.

This may be an all too familiar scene if a substantial disaster occurs where services and infrastructure essentials cannot be restored. Scavenging for supplies will become commonplace, with dangers for scavengers and defenders alike. Photo courtesy of www.pixabay.com.

Some will die instantly from the direct result of a catastrophic weather event or a thermo-nuclear detonation. Others will die from violent attack, as desperate, ill-prepared people will forcibly take supplies and items remaining on the store shelves. Still others will succumb to sicknesses and disease as a result of limited or non-existent health care. As the bodies pile up with fewer people able or willing to properly bury the dead, diseases once controlled and contained, will re-emerge back into the realm of epidemic certainty. This will further increase the body count.

Signs like this may not be enough of a deterrent for desperate people. Photo courtesy of www.pixabay.com.

If an electromagnetic pulse or weather phenomenon takes down the power grid with no foreseeable restoration, more bodies will pile up. Those depending on gas and electricity for heating and sterilizing water will have a bleak and agonizingly short future. Depending on the time of year, exposure to extreme weather temperatures is a stark reality that challenges even the best-prepared and trained survivalists.

Your ultimate survival will depend on the possibility of renouncing some of your currently held beliefs about civility and the appropriation of goods after an apocalyptic type event. I am not advocating stealing or looting for the sake of taking supplies under the delusional guise of social justice and entitlement. Nor am I endorsing the behavior of the rogue marauder who intends on forcibly pilfering the stockpiles of those wise enough to prepare in advance.

No matter how prepared one may be for any cataclysmic event, the need to replenish supplies will be of vital importance. Sadly, consumables are just that, consumable. The longer services and supply chains remain disrupted, the faster one has to resort to scavenging and foraging. Regardless of where you search, you will want to take back as much as you can carry. You might not get another opportunity to come back to the same location. Someone else, either before you or after you, will try to gather the items that are considered to be of value. For this reason, you should prioritize your needs and the needs of others within your group.

Food, water, medical supplies, and hygiene items like toilet paper are of the highest value to most people. Even if you are well stocked in these items, take them as you can barter these for other necessities.

It should be of some note that rich, extravagant looking homes may not provide a large quantity of emergency stockpiles. This might be an enticing quest to journey into very affluent districts in search of supplies. However, opportunistic scavengers, especially the government-dependent poor, will believe the fallacy that the rich have everything they need. They want to hit the mother lode and maybe take over and become squatters in the first abandoned mansion they find. I'm not condemning them for having this type of mentality, but I certainly won't condone or encourage it.

Large homes like this may be tempting to explore for supplies. You must weigh the risks of both finding nothing or finding something you didn't bargain or prepare for because of poor scouting. Photo courtesy of www.pixabay.com.

These people are looking for the easy way, the path of least resistance, and even less work. This means there is a greater likelihood of coming in contact with other scavengers, who may or may not be more desperate. The more desperate the person may be, the greater the propensity for confrontation and potential violence.

Scavengers will not have the luxury of being choosey with availability or the condition of the limited resources. Photo courtesy of www.pixabay.com.

One of the greatest downfalls of rich people is their tendency to believe that money will always buy what they need, when they need it Oftentimes, it means that some of the richest people are also the most ill-prepared. Their food is usually fresh, catered, or prepared every day so canned goods in a pantry are commonly absent. Common staples might be present, but only the housekeeping and cooking staff will truly know what is on hand and in ample supply. The domiciled elitist is often too busy, too self-absorbed, or too oblivious to manage and maintain emergency food supplies.

Survival rations will be a rude awakening for most wealthy and affluent people. Freeze-dried rations and MREs will be far from what is normally considered palatable table fare.

Some folks are fortunate to come into great sums of wealth. This wealth provides them with options. Many choose to build custom homes, which may include whole rooms that are not detectable. They have no need to hide little amounts of valuables throughout their homes. Their homes are further protected by guard dogs or alarm systems that keep the casual burglar away. High-society and elitists have the luxury of the aforementioned deterrents, in addition to armed guards, roving patrols, and state-of-the-art anti-intrusion systems similar to those used by banks and jewelry stores.

For the rest of society, however, they must stash their treasures and trinkets where they can. My grandparents, who lived through the Great Depression, often quoted the popular mantra of that era, "Save what you can and can what you save."

Many people will scavenge and collect instant consumables first to restock depleted supplies or maybe even eat something substantial for the first time in weeks. The average human can survive only about three weeks without food.

Instant consumables can be any of, but not limited to the following examples:

Bottled water
Pre-packaged food (MREs and freeze-dried food)
Canned goods
Staple foods
Staple ingredients (flour, sugar, grains, pasta, rice)
Salt
Spices
Fuel
Alcohol
Firewood
Matches
Candles
Batteries
Paper
Writing utensils (pens, pencils, chalk)
Charcoal
Chlorine bleach (liquid or powdered, i.e. pool shock)
Ammunition
Soap
Personal hygiene items
Toilet paper
Seeds
Canning lids

Durable consumables are the second group of items to catch the eye of scavengers. These items are often reusable or repurposed after the original purpose has lapsed or is intended for repeated use.

These include:

Buckets and containers (food-grade being highly sought after)
Books (especially manuals, DIY, and how-to books)
Glassware
Tools
Cleaning equipment
Tires
Scrap metal
Kitchen utensils
Canning supplies
Clothing
Textiles and fabrics
Furniture
PVC pipe
Firearms
Reloading supplies
Building materials
Backpacks
Carts/wagons
Playing cards/games
Plastic or Canvas bags
Planters and gardening supplies
Automobile parts
Bricks and concrete blocks
Fencing

Items once regarded as throw-away may indeed become a high demand commodity. Worn-out things or items that no longer work in their intended capacity will be repurposed, or used despite its limited effectiveness to accomplish its original design and purpose.

Almost anything and everything can be modified, reused, or repurposed to accomplish tasks that maintain your survival. Photo courtesy of www.pixabay.com.

Look at the preceding photo and see how many different items could be used to store or hide other items. What items could be used for their original purpose? Which items could be repurposed or modified for another purpose?

Questions such as these will aid you in reaping the greatest benefits in a survival situation. Make use of every possible thing you can to help yourself or others within your group.

Final Thoughts

It is my true desire that several portions of the information presented in this book will never have to be put into practice on a wide scale. However, neither men nor governments can be fully trusted, so prepare in the best ways you deem necessary for your survival.

I also highly recommend seeking out reputable survival training programs which include primitive skill elements, as well as training programs for self-defense, various weapon platforms, SERE, urban survival, scout and reconnaissance training, first-aid, herbal medicine, and self-sustainable living.

Appendix - Case Law Examples

<u>Disclaimer:</u> The following case law examples deal with search and seizures. A brief explanation is listed with each case, but it the responsibility of the reader to look up the full court opinion on any particular case. This brief listing does not constitute any inferred legal advice, but does provide relevance to the subject matter of this book. No intentional copyright infringement is intended under the guidelines of Fair Use laws.

Johnson v. United States, 333 U. S. 10, 333 U. S. 13-14 (1948) - Inconvenience to the police officers is no excuse for circumventing the Constitutional requirements of the Fourth Amendment. There were also no exigent circumstances in this case. Therefore, the officers should have obtained a search warrant.

US v. Jeffers, 342 U.S. 48 (1951) - Occupants of a hotel room have an expectation of privacy. An officer cannot freely enter and search a hotel room for contraband or evidence, nor can hotel staff grant permission for the police to enter and search the occupied room. The officer must follow the same procedures as if the room was a residence (i.e. obtain a search warrant, get consent, or have exigent circumstances). The court also added that a person has no right to have contraband, even if illegally seized, returned to him.

Camara v. Municipal Court, 387 U.S. 523 (1967) - Administrative inspections by Municipal Fire, Health, Home Inspection, or other similar agencies require a search warrant if the occupant of a residence refuses to allow the inspection.

Shipley v. California, 395 U.S. 818 (1969) - The police cannot do a search incident to arrest of the suspect's home if the suspect is arrested outside the residence.

US v. Robinson, 430 F.2d 1141 (6th Cir. 1970) - A person has no expectation of privacy in a home, hotel room, vehicle, etc. if he abandoned it.   The police have a heavy burden of proof in establishing that the person abandoned the property. The mere fact that the defendant was arrested and imprisoned did not meet the burden of whether he intended to abandon the property.

Michigan v. Tyler, 436 US 499 (1978) - "A burning building clearly presents an exigency of sufficient proportions to render a warrantless entry "reasonable," and, once in the building to extinguish a blaze, and for a reasonable time thereafter, firefighters may seize evidence of arson that is in plain view and investigate the causes of the fire."

Michigan v. Clifford, 464 US 287 (1984) - A person does not lose his expectation of privacy in his home when the home is destroyed by fire. The initial entry into the home to extinguish the fire and contemporaneous investigation into the cause of the fire is justified as an exigency of the fire, (Michigan v. Tyler). The fire marshal started his investigation several hours after the fire was extinguished. This break in time and lack of exigency meant the marshal was required to gain consent or a warrant to enter the premises to investigate the cause of the fire.

Payton v. New York, 445 US 573 (1980) - A warrant based on probable cause is required to arrest a felon inside a private home. The only exception is under exigent circumstances.

Steagald v. U.S. 451 US 204 (1981) - Absent a consent or exigent circumstances, a search warrant is needed to arrest someone from the home of a third party.

Illinois v. Andreas, 463 U.S. 765 (1983) - "If an inspection by police does not intrude upon a legitimate expectation of privacy, there is no "search" subject to the Warrant Clause. No protected privacy interest remains in contraband in a container once government officers lawfully (as here) have opened that container and identified its contents as illegal. The simple act of resealing the container to enable the police to make a controlled delivery does not operate to revive or restore the lawfully invaded privacy rights, and the subsequent reopening of the container is not a "search" within the intendment of the Fourth Amendment." It is irrelevant that the container leaves the control or view of the police for a brief period. The warrantless seizure is permissible. In this case, the defendant took possession for about 35 minutes. He left his home and he and the container were seized. The container was lawfully re-opened without a warrant. The time period is governed by whether there is a "substantial likelihood" that the contents of the container changed during the surveillance gap.

Bledsoe v. Garcia, 742 F. 2d 1237 (10th Cir. 1984)-Bledsoe was contacted in front of his parents' house by police. The officer also asked him if he was AWOL. Bledsoe admitted that he knew he was. The officer told him that he was being arrested. Bledsoe asked and was granted permission to enter his home to tell his parents. The parents refused to let him go with the police and interfered with the police when they entered to arrest Bledsoe. The court held that AWOL was a serious offense justifying the entry of the home and search for Bledsoe.

Minnesota v. Olson, 495 US 91 (1990) - The overnight guest at another's dwelling does have an expectation of privacy. The Steagald case applies. Olson was the driver of the getaway car used in a robbery and murder. He took refuge at a friend's house. The police entered the residence without a warrant and arrested him. He was questioned and made some admissions. The arrest was ruled to be illegal. The admissions were excluded.

Minnesota v. Carter, 525 US 83 (1998) - Defendants had no Fourth Amendment Protection. Even though they were observed in illegal activity through a crack in the blind of a private home, they had no expectation of privacy. Respondents were obviously not overnight guests, but were essentially present for a business transaction and were only in the home for a matter of hours. There was nothing to suggest that they had a previous relationship with the owner or that there was any other purpose to their visit. While the apartment was a dwelling place for the occupant, for the defendants, it was simply a place to do business.

Flippo v. West Virginia, 528 US 11(1999) - The search of a murder scene without a warrant caused problems in court. There is not a general "murder exception" to the warrant requirement of the Fourth Amendment. The constitutionally mandated rules of search and seizure do not generally change based upon the seriousness of the offense. In crimes where the suspect may have a reasonable expectation of privacy in the scene, officers must be ever mindful of the warrant requirement.

Wilson v. Layne, 000 US 98-83 (1999) - The Fourth Amendment rights of homeowners are violated when police bring members of the media or other third parties into their home during the execution of a warrant. The third parties presence in the home was not to aid in the execution of the warrant for it to be a violation, however.

US v. Gay, 451 US 204 (10th Cir, 2001) - A police officer only needs to reasonably believe that a person lives at a particular residence at the time of entry to arrest on a warrant.

Illinois v. McArthur, 531 U.S. 326 (2001) - A police officer's two-hour restraint of a homeowner while a search warrant was being obtained was reasonable. The court noted that the officer had probable cause to believe there was evidence of a crime and reasonably believed that the evidence would be destroyed if the resident were left alone. Further, the police made a diligent effort to obtain the warrant as quickly as possible.

Kyllo v. US, 000 US 99-8508(2001) - The government use of a thermal imaging device, a device not in general public use, to explore details of a private home that would previously have been unknowable without physical intrusion, is a Fourth Amendment "search," and is unreasonable without a warrant.

US v. Knights, 000 US 00-1260 (2001) - Knights was sentenced to probation for a drug offense. A condition of his probation included that he submit to search at anytime, with or without a search or arrest warrant or reasonable cause, by any probation or law enforcement officer. A sheriff's detective searched Knights' apartment based on reasonable suspicion. He found evidence of crime for which Knight was indicted. The search was reasonable because Knight had a diminished expectation of privacy.

Gonzales v. Raich, 000 U.S. 03-1454 (2005) - The Federal Government has the authority to prevent states from legalizing the use of marijuana for medical purposes.

Coffin v. Brandau, 642 F.3d 999 (11th Cir. 2011) - Police are not permitted to enter into someone's garage when that person is closing it to maintain his/her privacy. In this case, the homeowner pushed the button to close the powered garage door. The officer put his foot in the electric safety beam by the door to prevent the door from closing. The officer entered the garage. This violated the owner's 4th Amendment rights.

United States v. Creighton, 639 F.3d 1281 (10th Cir. 2011) - "Although a motel guest does have a legitimate expectation of privacy in his room, *United States v. Gordon, 168 F.3d 1222, 1225–26* (10th Cir. 1999), that expectation of privacy is lost when the rental period for the room expires. *United States v. Croft, 429 F.2d 884, 887* (10th Cir. 1970); . . . "Since after the rental period expires a guest has no right of privacy, there can be no invasion thereof." *Croft, 429 F.2d at 887*."

Mascorro v. Billings, 10-7005 (10th Cir. 2011) - A police officer saw a known juvenile pass him at night without functioning taillights. The officer turned to stop the vehicle. The driver drove two blocks to his home and ran inside before the officer could catch and stop him. The officer forced his way in against the consent of the parents pepper spraying them in the process. The juvenile was found and arrested in the bathroom. The Court held that an officer must have:

1.   A serious offense, and
2.   An exigent circumstance

Both of these must occur before an officer can enter a home and make an arrest without a warrant.   In this case, a minor traffic offense was not serious and did not justify the warrantless entry and arrest.   A serious offense can be either a felony or misdemeanor.   Either one, however, must have a very strong justification.   A DUI charge does not meet the criteria, see *Welch v. Wisconsin*, but AWOL does see *Bledsoe v. Garcia*.

US v. Wells, 11-5162 (10th Cir. 2011) - Tulsa police officers were suspected of stealing from drug dealers.   A sting operation was set up where the officers were told of a drug dealer with a lot of cash take was staying in a motel.   An undercover officer posing as the dealer rented the room and installed surveillance equipment.   The officers contacted the dealer and obtained consent to search.   The officers entered the room without the dealer and stole several thousand dollars.   The officers were arrested.   They fought to suppress the recordings claiming that they had an expectation of privacy.   The Court held that the officers were not invited guests, but merely legally in the room.   They had no expectation of privacy.   The recordings were admissible.

US v. Nora, No. 12-50485 (9th Cir 2014) - Officers saw Nora standing on the sidewalk by his house.   As they approached him, he had moved to his porch.   The officers saw a handgun in his hand.   He entered his house and shut the door.   The officers called for backup.   Over twenty officers surrounded his house and a helicopter watched from above.   The officers ordered him out of the house at gunpoint.   They arrested him for the misdemeanor offense of carrying a firearm in public.   The officers did not know Nora or that he had a felony conviction at the time of arrest.   They searched him and found drugs. They questioned him. He admitted to more drugs being in the house.   The officers got a warrant and searched his house.   They found distribution quantity of cocaine, methamphetamine, and numerous firearms in the house.   The Court held that Nora was unlawfully arrested out of his house in violation of Payton v. New York. It was a minor offense and there were no exigent circumstances justifying the warrantless arrest from his home. The drugs found on him and his statement was excluded. The officers did not name specifically in the search warrant that they were looking for the pistol they saw Nora with. The search warrant only mentioned any firearm. The Court invalidated the entire search warrant.

Moore v. Pederson, No. 14-14201 (11th Cir 2015) - Under the Fourth Amendment, the home is a sacrosanct place that enjoys special protection from government intrusion. The government may not enter a person's home to effect an arrest without a warrant, or probable cause plus either consent or exigent circumstances.

US v. Thompson, No. 15-2008 (7th Cir. 2016) - The court held that an informant for the police, when invited into a home, can secretly video record the interior of the home.

Morse v. Cloutier, No. 15-2043 (1st Cir. 2017) - Morse was throwing bottles and other dangerous objects at his neighbors. He also threatened to kill them. Morse returned to his home and was contacted there approximately one hour later by several police officers. They contacted him as he stood behind his locked storm door. The officers asked him to step outside. He refused. An officer told him he was under arrest. Morse told the officer he needed a warrant and shut and locked the inner door. The officers forced open the doors, entered Morse's residence, and arrested him. Morse and his wife sued the officers for violating their civil rights for breaking into his home to arrest him without a warrant in violation of his 4th Amendment rights. The lower court and Court of Appeals denied the officers qualified immunity because the law was clearly established forbidding what they did.

Source:
http://www.caselaw4cops.net/searchandseizure/homes.htm

Additional resources:

Angelo, *Prisoner Inventions*, Whitewalls, Inc., 2003

Brindle, Damian, *75 of the Best Secret Hiding Places: How to Outsmart Thieves Using Hidden Safes, Secret Compartments, and More*, Amazon Digital Services, LLC, 2018

Cobb, Jim, *Prepper's Home Defense: Security Strategies to Protect Your Family by Any Means Necessary*, Ulysses Press, 2012

Cobb, Jim, *Prepper's Long-Term Survival Guide*, Ulysses Press, 2014

Connor, Michael, *How to Hide Anything*, Paladin Press, 1984

Dzindzeleta, Jerry, *Secret Rooms, Secret Compartments*, self-published, 1990

Eddie the Wire, *How to Bury Your Goods: The Complete Manual of Long-Term underground Storage*, Paladin Press, 1999

Fiery, Dennis, *How to Hide Things in Public Places*, Breakout Productions, 2001

Krotz, David, *How to Hide Almost Anything*, Morrow, 1975

Luger, Jack, *The Big Book of Secret Hiding Places*, Breakout Productions, 1987

Nobody, Joe & Pike, T., *The Prepper's Guide to Caches: How to Bury, Hide, and Stash Guns and Gear*, Prepper Press, 2015

Plant, Steve, *DIY: Secret Hiding Places: 90 Places to Hide What You Don't Want Found*, CreateSpace Independent Publishing Platform, 2016

Rayder, Steve, *The Prepper's Apocalypse Survival Guide to Scavenging Everyday Household Items*, CreateSpace Independent Publishing Platform, 2015

Robinson, Charles, *Construction of Secret Hiding Places*, Desert Publications, 1981

Trubble, Tristan, *101 Secret Hiding Places*, CreateSpace Independent Publishing Platform, 2016

Websites:

www.SecretStashSafes.com
www.happypreppers.com
www.diversionsafesworld.com
www.spygearflorida.com
www.amazon.com
www.homeselfdefenseproducts.com
www.pinterest.com
www.ebay.com
www.personalsecuritystore.com
www.spynuts.com
www.stashit.net
www.toledoguardian.com
www.reveresecurity.com
www.diversion-safes.com
www.stashvault.com
www.selfdefenseproducts.com
www.stashsafewarehouse.com
www.thesafesleuth.com
www.mind4survival.com
www.survivalweekly.com
www.americanpreppersnetwork.com
www.survivalblog.com
www.secretstorages.com
www.stealthfurniture.com
www.libertyhomeconcealment.com
www.hiddendoorstore.com
www.tacticalwalls.com
www.njconceal.co
www.ultimatesecuritydevices.com

About the Author

Matthew Dermody is the author of four other books about camouflage and concealment. He currently resides in Perth, Australia with his wife and their twin girls.

He is a US Navy veteran, serving 6 years as a Cryptologic Technician (maintenance) specializing in shipboard and shore site communications systems and physical security equipment. He has worked as an alarm installer and technician, armed courier driver, and security guard positions.

He has a Criminal Justice degree and recently obtained his Western Australia Certificate II & III in Security Operations.

Other Published Works

Books:
Hidden Success: A Comprehensive Guide to Ghillie Suit Construction
Appear to Vanish: Stealth Concepts for Effective Camouflage and Concealment
Gray Man: Camouflage for Crowds, Cities, and Civil Crisis
Gray Woman: A Woman's Guide to Gray Man Tactics (e-book)
Conversational Camouflage: Oratory Discretion and Pretexting for Behavioral Concealment

Website Resources: (hiddensuccesstactical.com)
Civilian and Military Camouflage Patterns – General Editor
Inexpensive Winter Ghillie Blanket
3 Reasons to Stock up on Halloween Make-Up
The Tactical Drawbacks of High-Definition (HD) Camouflage Patterns

Guest Blogs:
Six Materials for Field Expedient Natural Camouflage –
www.willowhavenoutdoor.com
Do You Really Need a Ghillie Suit? – www.itstactical.com
Build Your Own Ghillie Suit for Under $75 – www.itstactical.com
Practical Alternatives for Buried Survival Caches –
www.survivalschool.us

9 781717 492029